KALEIDOSCOPE

DERBY

Edited by Allison Dowse

First published in Great Britain in 1999 by
POETRY NOW YOUNG WRITERS
Remus House,
Coltsfoot Drive,
Woodston,
Peterborough, PE2 9JX
Telephone (01733) 890066

HB ISBN 0 75430 708 5
SB ISBN 0 75430 709 3

FOREWORD

This year, the Poetry Now Young Writers' Kaleidoscope competition proudly presents the best poetic contributions from over 32,000 up-and-coming writers nationwide.

Successful in continuing our aim of promoting writing and creativity in children, each regional anthology displays the inventive and original writing talents of 11-18 year old poets. Imaginative, thoughtful, often humorous, *Kaleidoscope Derby* provides a captivating insight into the issues and opinions important to today's young generation.

The task of editing inevitably proved challenging, but was nevertheless enjoyable thanks to the quality of entries received. The thought, effort and hard work put into each poem impressed and inspired us all. We hope you are as pleased as we are with the final result and that you continue to enjoy *Kaleidoscope Derby* for years to come.

CONTENTS

Deborah Hill	67
Kelly Morgan	68
Claire Southam	69
Anastasia Hagan	70
Thomas Oakley	71
Emma Newstead	72
Rebecca Gray	73
Tesney Swann	74
Amy Spencer	75
Holly Barlow	76
Martin Simpson	77
Jamie Birkin	78
Michael Siviter	79
Michelle Cain	80
James Hassall	81
Asim Rashid	82
Jenny Thorpe	83

Murray Park School

Simon Inman	84
Kavita Rawal	85
Sarah Lauder	86
Hardeep Nanuwan	87
Amber Collinge	88

Noel Baker Community School

Alison Blood	89
Daniel Hamilton	90
Katy Heron	91
Alex Whyman	92
Andrew Pell	93
Laura Wilkinson	94
Johnathan Bousfield	95
Samantha Cooper	96
Emma Hollis	97
Stacy Lowe	98
Liam Birch	99
Charlotte Brown	100

The Poems

UNTITLED

I hear crying in a room
full of sadness
full of gloom.
If I could touch one little tear.
He would never feel anymore fear.

Jenny Cartwright

NEWSPAPER

Black and white
but in colour
it's a hat, a boat or a fire.

Sometimes it's just read
sometimes it's a lining
for a cat's bed.

It's made in mass production
it's thrown away in tonnes.

With some flour and water
you can make anything.

Newspaper
Newspaper
Oh! What a wonderful thing!

Emma Thirkill (14)
Bemrose Community School

THE COUNTRY COTTAGE

I'm alone in the countryside - nobody nearby.
You can come inside when it's cold and sit beside
the warm log fire.
You can sit on the cold stone floor and listen
to Grandma reading a sweet short story.
Then you go to a warm cosy bed.
Then you wake up to the sound of the cockerel.
You all then sit round the big pine table
eating bacon and egg.
After that you're in the field to feed the animals
in their pens - then it starts all over again.

Arran Wilson (14)
Bemrose Community School

SUMMER POEM

Summer is beautiful
sun shining bright,
daisies, buttercups everywhere
you look.

Everyone is on the beach swimming
in the sea.
Summer, summer - it's the best.

Hot, hot - everyone has ice cubes
in their drinks.
Birds flying in the light blue sky.

I love the summer holidays
because there is no school.
Camping is fun in the sun,
in the rain it's not so good.
The rain never comes down
when the sun's out.
Most people get sunburnt in the summer.

Linda Jordan (12)
Bemrose Community School

MANCHESTER UNITED FOOTBALL CLUB

Manchester United have a very talented team
from attackers to mid-fielders
from defenders to the goalkeeper
from the olden days to the present day.
They still play with passion
so fierce, so skilled, they're a hard team to beat.
Alex Ferguson manages the team.
Old Trafford is magnificent, but I've never been.
They have done Newton Heath proud - very proud indeed
but there is a sad story to tell.
The Munich air disaster,
where we had to say goodbye to most of the Busby Babes.
It always brings tears to my eyes
but now we have fully recovered.
We've got some of the finest players in the world.
Peter Schmeichel, Ole Gunnar Solskjaer,
David Beckham and Ryan Giggs.
I just hope nothing happens to *these* babes.

Shelley Shepherd (13)
Bemrose Community School

A LITTLE BOY WHO IS CRYING FOR FOOD AND HELP

My life is dirty there is nothing to eat.
All I do is sit and wait for my next meal to come.
I shout in the middle of the streets
'I beg you let me have a single coin.'
They push me over like I'm nothing.

My mother and father were killed
and I've nobody to care for me now.
Oh how I wish they were alive!
All I have on is a tatty pair of pants
and I'm hungry!
I shout for ages but nobody hears me
I break down in tears.

I've got no choice, I must steal
- it's wrong, but I'm hungry!
For a living I wash about a 100 cars a day
trying to earn money.
It makes me want to cry when I'm so tired
but I still work because I'm so hungry.

My bed is nothing but a cardboard box
which is small, but I have to make do.
Before I go to sleep I pray to God;
if anybody can hear me please give me food
and a nice home.

Amen.

Linval O'Connor (13)
Bemrose Community School

VIEW FROM ABOVE

The rounded sphere, so particular in shape.
With distinguished yet fused colours.
No obvious movement,
except for the white fluffy cottony misshapes.
Giant hand, cold eruptions poking from inside
like a Busby hat standing proud.
Plates of ore on a blue bed
like oil, floating on water.
Millions of dots, scurrying around
like termites sculpting a mould.
But one day when all is gone
will it go bang?
Or will its light slowly burn out?
Like a candle in the wind.

Gavin Quenby (13)
Bemrose Community School

IF I CLOSE MY EYES AND THINK

If I close my eyes and think
I think about the starving children
they're always working hard for little pay.
I wish I could help those in the Third World.

If I close my eyes and think
I think about the victims of violence and crime.
What did they do to deserve it?
I wish I could help them.

In this world, there is plenty of room for improvement.
Every single country should work together
in perfect harmony.

Richard Wheatley (13)
Bemrose Community School

THE TERROR OF NIGHT

I walk alone
My path is unsure.
I walk through the dark
I see them there.
There's nowhere to hide
I try and scream.
No sound
I'm alone
No one to find
I try and run
My feet are lead
Then I awake
I am safe in my bed.

Kerry O'Gara (13)
Bemrose Community School

THE EARTHQUAKE

Rolling rumbling earthquake.
Shattering and smashing houses and buildings all around.
They run for help
They panic and scream
The people . . .
They're trapped beneath the shamble of houses.
They're trapped beneath the bricks and soil.
Who can help them? Who can save them?
No one knows . . .
They all run away
frightened to death.
The people . . .
Don't want to save them.
Afraid of getting trapped.
Left there -
Alone and forgotten.
Till your blood grows cold
And small hope begins to fade.
And slowly - ever so slowly
You die there.
All on your own . . .

Seika Rafiq (13)
Bemrose Community School

A POEM ABOUT CLOUDS

Clouds are white in the sky in the
     blueness up
          so high.

Floating round like a boat on the sea

Flying round like a honeybee.

You would fall straight through
     them because they're
          so soft and light.

In the pale moonlight you can see
     the fading shapes.

Samantha Wesson (12)
Bemrose Community School

KOALA

Ears so cute and fluffy
just a cot in winter.
Trees sway in the cool night breeze
body trembling like leaves.
Eyes twinkling in the pale moonlight.
Heart as warm as an angels.
Climbing, climbing, wanting, needing, waiting . . .

Jade Cooper (12)
Bemrose Community School

THE NIGHT HAS A THOUSAND EYES

The night has a thousand eyes
all lit up in the black skies.
Twinkling like gems in the night
unable to touch - only to see.
The five-pointed yellow images
standing out in the heavy darkness.
These are stars shining brightly
like a thousand eyes in the night.

Lisa Yeomans (12)
Bemrose Community School

WHAT AM I?

When finished raining
I come out.
You can see me in the sky
I am bright and beautiful
I have seven colours on me
I can't do anything
But look pretty
What am I . . . ?

Jenny Mo (13)
Bemrose Community School

A KANGAROO

The sun beats down on the ground
he knows that he has just been found
He gets pointed at - with a shiny gun
he stands there in fright with nowhere
to run.
The bullet fires at the kangaroo
Bang! He's dead . . .
Nothing he could do.

Michael Nagy (12)
Bemrose Community School

SPIDERS

Spiders are furry and have eight legs
with beady eyes on their heads.
As they run along the ground in a scurry
running after their prey in a hurry.
Tarantula - so big and hairy.
They look at you, it's almost scary.
When they sleep hanging upside down at night
When they hear a sound they're in fright.
Spiders climbing up the wall
and crawling fast across the kitchen floor.
When I'm asleep I feel the spiders in the room
and in my bed.
I wish, I wish - they were dead!

Ashlee Higgins (12)
Bemrose Community School

RAIN

I was sitting down and thinking
the dripping rain started and my eyes
started to twinkle.
I was sad and alone
the doorbell rang and I jumped
up and it made me happy.

Twinkle, twinkle eyes
with rain pouring in the sky.
Twinkle, twinkle eyes
with tears coming out.
Sad and alone sitting next
to the window.
Twinkle, twinkle eyes
and sitting and thinking
about life and future.

Make other people happy
who are sad and need your help.
And don't think about yourself
stay happy but never sad.

Nagina Ali (14)
Bemrose Community School

KANGAROO

She keeps her family in her pouch
Bounding merrily through the air
Shout her name and she will not stop
What she has she will not drop.

Afzal Araf (13)
Bemrose Community School

SCHOOL AT HOME

Homework is increasing
It seems to drive me nuts
There is more and more each day there seems
And even heavier books.

With getting worked so hard
It seems a bit blasé
That teachers give us homework overnight
To hand in the next day.

Teachers then complain about
The quality of our work
But not having time to think it through
Doesn't help of course.

Teachers had this in the past
I'm sure they understand
But if they went through this
Then why so much homework planned?

Joanna Turner (14)
Bemrose Community School

PAINTING WITH HER!

'We want to paint some pictures!'
we say to our mum.
Wear your oldest clothes
and have a lot of fun.

We go into the garden and sit beside a tree.
My sister paints a snail, I paint three.
She got yellow paint over her dress
then spilled the water and made a big mess!

She then thinks it's fun to dip her fingers in paint
and flicks them at everyone.

I scream and run, then trip into my dad
who's sleeping
and he just might get mad!

He wakes up with a grin, we laugh and run.
Leaving paper, paints and brushes
for dad to bring in today.

Much later - me and my sister creep back
when mum calls.
'Come and see your paintings,
we've hung them on the walls.'

The love and bond we sometimes have
is a very meaningful thing.
So if you have a little one
try not to be mean!

Danielle Roche (13)
Bemrose Community School

RED

The evil fox in the woods.
Like the devil from Manchester United,
Eric the red is his name.
An English rose shredded to bits,
Blood is everywhere,
Shiny as a tomato.
As ripe as an apple,
As seedless as a strawberry,
Blood Angels claim victory.
The fire spreads,
Phone boxes ring
The tower collapses
Into the deadly pit of doom.
Celebrating death,
Red wine is drunk
In hell!
Red is evil
Red is bad
Red is definitely sinful.

Kris Taylor (13)
Derby Independent Grammar School for Boys

RED

A flickering flame destroys another building.
Molten lava flows from another body.
Terracotta dust rises from destroyed bricks.
Fiery bright fire engines arrive
Coke cans explode with fury.

Telephone boxes are never quiet.
There are rosy-cheeked women.
The outstanding, active cross goes to another
War-torn country.
Arsenal come off the pitch crimson with sweat.

Tom Alcock (13)
Derby Independent Grammar School for Boys

RED

The sun sets at eight o'clock
as red as a fiery hell.
When the devil falls down
the darkness will be upon us.
My body is sore,
however he has gone for now.
The devil has been stinging me
with his red hot fork.
Like a poker in the fire
it glows with fury.
I have caught the rash
of its infectious disease.
Hurry up winter and come
so then the devil will be gone.

Robert Lawson (14)
Derby Independent Grammar School for Boys

KALEIDOSCOPE

Your existence is a kaleidoscope of
situations, money and colours.
Your school, your university, your job
are a kaleidoscope of knowledge and colours.
Your exams, your hopes, your dreams,
are a kaleidoscope of worries and colours.
Your job, your family, your home,
are a kaleidoscope of caring and colours.
Your ancestors, your grandchildren, your great grandchildren,
are a kaleidoscope of history and colours.
Your birth, your life, your death
are a kaleidoscope of confusion and
changes.

Ben Holmes (13)
Derby Independent Grammar School for Boys

KALEIDOSCOPE

Kaleidoscope;
Always changing
Like patterns in the flames;
Ever turning, tumbling and
I nterweaving;
Dazzling colours
Of every hue,
Shade, tint and tone
Coming together to make
Original designs; moving
Perpetually, never static;
Either a face, fireworks, or a flower, or . . .

Andrew Allcorn (13)
Derby Independent Grammar School for Boys

ORANGE

A ball of brightness
Illuminating the morning
Burning frantically.
The sweltering heat of Orange County.
Watching the inspiring, creative football of Holland,
While dull, dirty carrots lie underground.
Huge, ripe, succulent oranges.
Bright balloons float in the air,
Watching the sun's rays illuminate the morning.

Chris Waddy (13)
Derby Independent Grammar School for Boys

LIGHT BLUE

A slippery surface on the road,
transparent like a pane of glass.
Pebbles of ice falling from the sky
people hurrying, hurrying past.
The cold north wind whistling down the road,
past the postman collecting his Christmas letters.
The fingers of Jack Frost
rubbing over my face, my hands, my ears.
Frost-bitten lips yearning for a cup of tea.
Longing to sit next to a warm glowing fire
covered by a loving blanket.
People wanting to fill up their hot water bottles,
and crawl slowly back to the safety of their beds.
They drift away dreaming of a colour,
and it's called *light blue* . . .

Alex Gill (12)
Derby Independent Grammar School for Boys

BLACK 'N' WHITE

Staring up into the starry night sky
brilliant white specks in the vast blackness.
Black and white pieces
on a chequered-board.
A very old photo, 1940's or so;
The magpies dance in the country fields
just around the corner to a newspaper shop.
All the days' headlines stacked up in a pile.
Two bright lights moving swiftly closer.
The screeching of brakes, marks left on the road.
Looking down the motorway
the millions of cat's eyes: staring.

Tom Ward (13)
Derby Independent Grammar School for Boys

GREEN

The flower stood proud and honourable in the beautiful garden.
The sunshine helped the growth of the mighty flower.
Every year this flower blossomed and emerged from the earth.
Nothing on earth could bring down God's being.

The growing plants look good in the small and beautiful gardens.
Like flocks of honourable soldiers going to war.
So strong and sturdy.
No one could kill God's beings.

There are the cultivated fruits in that orchard.
So grand like city buildings in Japan.
When watched, look as robust as ever.
No one can harm God's beings.

There stood the evil weeds.
So cowardly and sneakily they grow.
They do not care what havoc they cause.
Everyone wants to kill this being of God's
Why?

Rakesh Rao (13)
Derby Independent Grammar School for Boys

RED

Juicy strawberry flat on my tongue
All squashed.
Cherry-red cheeks of the embarrassed boy.
Roses smelling delicious.
The teenagers by the telephone box;
A rocket ship about to be launched.
Blood smelling like a cold winter's day.
Red devil comes out when all dark and gloomy.
Sneaks around until light, wondering what to eat.
The fire was as hot as chilli powder.

Thomas Holmes (13)
Derby Independent Grammar School for Boys

RED

As crimson as bricks
on a rainy day.
Glowing with anger,
pain, blood, fire.
As flaming as United,
with a devil on their shirt.

The hot molten lava spitting slowly
makes me think of fire.
Brake-lights on a foggy day
shine like the sun.
As fiery as the rose
on the England shirt.

Rahul Sharma (13)
Derby Independent Grammar School for Boys

DREAMS OF THE NIGHT SKY

As I look into the starlit sky
high above the birds that fly.
I see the stars all glowing bright
exploding like some dynamite.

How I wonder what it's like
to be up there, a star in flight.
Oh how wondrous it would be
rising, falling, it's so free.

Suddenly the clouds draw in,
the stars have gone, the sky is dim.
The dream I had to be so free
has rapidly backfired on me.

Jonathan Alvis (15)
Derby Independent Grammar School for Boys

NIGHT-TIME EAGLE

Like darkness rising, soaring
the night-time eagle.
On the prowl
devouring all in its path.

With silent grace it glides
smothering, engulfing all around.
The distant cry of the wolf's howl echoes
as darkness swoops upon the ground.

Like predator to prey
the eagle attacks.
The prey is the earth
the hunter the night.

David Wood (13)
Derby Independent Grammar School for Boys

KALEIDOSCOPE

As I twist and turn they appear
Lots of colours flying at me.
The colours mingle like a rainbow
With different shapes to see.

The patterns they form
Different with every turn.

The red is like fire - glowing and bright.
The blue is the ocean and sky in sight.
The green is like grass and trees that sway
Purple and orange shining at me.

Lines, swirling, slipping and sliding
Fragile, fleeting like the path of life.

Shaun Pickering (14)
Derby Independent Grammar School for Boys

KALEIDOSCOPE

When I look in my kaleidoscope what do I see?
A myriad of hues looking back at me.

The browns, fawns are dusty plains
The arrid landscape of Africa.

Glistening jades, pulsating terrain
Endless emeralds of rainforest.

Silver mirrored towers,
Reflects the greys and mauves : life in Hong Kong.

Red, blue, pink flashing 24 hours a day
the persistent neon lights of America.

Seen here is the world as a whole
where everything has a colour and everything a soul.

So in my kaleidoscope there are many images to view
step a little closer and they will become clear to you.

Christopher Bevan (13)
Derby Independent Grammar School for Boys

The Festival: A Kaleidoscope Of Colour

The sun hovers overhead
The stalls are out
The tables laid
And even the birds are gathered.

The crown looks on excitedly
The drums roll,
The trumpets sound.
So everything living can hear.

Suddenly, all life breaks free
The colour pours out.
In drenching sheets,
And even the blind can see.

The dresses are twirling
Their royal gold
Their reds and pinks
And even the puritan's smile.

Gaiety conquers far and wide
An ev'r changing scene.
Of colour and fun,
So unpredictable.

The performers disappear round the corner,
The colour gone,
The music faded,
And all that is left is the memory.

Arran Johnston (13)
Derby Independent Grammar School for Boys

KALEIDOSCOPE

I turn the wheel; a blue and green sparkle.
The deep orange sun leads the evening to darkle.
The next colourful pattern is there to please;
A butterfly, fluttering by in the morning breeze.

Another turn and the colours all mingle;
The waves all crash in and they cover the shingle.
Every scene is different on my kaleidoscope.
A steep mountain-face, and a sleeping antelope.

Another quick spin forms a maple leaf
Crunching through the meadows on the straw underneath.
My eye re-focuses and now I can see
A squirrel scurrying down the trunk of the tree.

The bits and pieces crunch, and change their shape.
My daydream is over, and I re-awake.

Matthew Flint (15)
Derby Independent Grammar School for Boys

TIME: A PARADOX

Ever coming, always going
Never ceasing, never stopping
Sometimes flying, sometimes walking
It's always staying at a constant pace.

Mostly fearful, mostly gentle
Never something you can see
Mostly something unpredictable
But always staying at a constant pace.

Cause of death, cause of life
Cause of love, cause of strife
Master of every single thing
And always staying at a constant pace.

Never ever what it seems
Always something it has been
Sometimes evil, sometimes good
Always staying at a constant pace.

Gui Tran (13)
Derby Independent Grammar School for Boys

A Sunset On The Grand Canyon

On this clean, quiet and peaceful night,
I sit alone.
Watching as reds, oranges, and yellows are painted above me,
By a sun sinking into the horizon:
Another night begins on the Grand Canyon.
I close my eyes,
Thinking about the world,
And see that the sun almost sleeps.

The scene and calm brings to my mind many things:
My family, my life and the beauty that the creatures here live in.
Time freezes and I watch this serene and tranquil locus.
The light and heat fade away.
As the sun disappears over gargantuan rock,
Painting light and shadows with a broad brush,
The brush that both darkens and gives light to the world.

Whoever has been to this shrine is blessed,
With the knowledge of this spectacular scene.
That no film or camera can depict,
I sit here alone,
In a great moment in time,
Amidst the greatest beauty ever seen,
And I think this is the place I would like to die in.

Rahul Singhal (13)
Derby Independent Grammar School for Boys

KALEIDOSCOPE

From the fire comes mat black smoke,
it twists and twirls and
makes you choke.
Flames and smoke leap and flow
and make your face brightly glow.
As it spirals and twirls up high,
it looks like shapes flying by.
Faces and pictures come and go,
and alter shape as you blow.
As the fire dies down low, we see
the faces fade and go.
When it's dark and the fire has
parted, we know tomorrow it will
be restarted.

Thomas Webster (13)
Derby Independent Grammar School for Boys

THE SEASONAL KALEIDOSCOPE

As I peer through the eyepiece
I start to see,
more than just colours
it appears to me.

There's the sun in the sky
and grass on the ground.
These were the seasons
that I had found.

But the rain comes down
when summer makes way.
It dampens morale
I hate to say.

The trees become leafless
and the leaves blow away.
The squirrels are collecting
some nuts and some hay.

This is for the winter
when they are asleep,
Won't be missing the weather
the rain and the sleet.

Then the clouds do depart
with one final sigh.
And summer is here . . .
but it's all in my eye.

Ryan Maquire (13)
Derby Independent Grammar School for Boys

A KALEIDOSCOPE OF FEELINGS

I look through the lens and see faint patterns of orange and blue
which grow stronger, as does my excitement.
Slowly, the blue spreads and overwhelms the orange, giving birth
to a single spark of yellow which flows and dances, creating a
feeling of joy.
The colours grow yet stronger.
They hurry around, red, black, blue giving me a feeling
of intense anger, until at last they die . . .

All that is left are the murky greens and greys,
leaving me sad at the loss of the other colours.

I leave the feelings behind in the kaleidoscope,
wondering what my next journey will hold.

Ben Haytack (12)
Derby Independent Grammar School for Boys

WOLF - THE MURDERER

Snow is falling and the wolf awakes,
He howls to call his pack.
When united they go to hunt,
crawling cautiously up behind the victim.
Then pouncing silently,
and savagely they kill it
with their deadly fangs and their razor-sharp claws.
Daylight breaks!
The pack scatters!
But will stalk their prey another cold winter night.

Andrew Shapcott (12)
Derby Independent Grammar School for Boys

NIGHTMARE THE HORSE

Galloping through the night
Hooves crashing and thundering.
Its long mane makes you shiver with fright.

Neighing - or is that you screaming?
A gust of wind, as the *nightmare horse* comes
running past.
It gallops as you try to run away
hoping that you will wake to see another day.

You wake up sweating.
It gallops into the night.
It is the *nightmare horse!*

Ranjit Thaker (12)
Derby Independent Grammar School for Boys

ARROW THE EAGLE

Through the air
He hunts
All leaves fall
As he darts by.

Far through the forest
His mourning prey are heard
As he swiftly finds a new prey
To eat and hunt.

As life dies away
Many a close escape
He wants to hunt
Another prey.

He swoops through the air
Hunting his prey
To their shadowy death.

Simon Law (12)
Derby Independent Grammar School for Boys

TIGERS AND MOUNTAINS

Clouds; cumuluo-nimbus
Floating through the sky.
Meaningless messes of vapour
Rearrange before your eyes:

A tiger in the jungle
'It's just a cloud though!'
A steamship, ploughing through a sea,
'It's just a cloud though!'
A mountain, tall, unconquerable,
'It's just a cloud though!'
A piano, playing silent tunes,
'It's just a cloud . . . ' No!

No.
I know they're only vapours,
Just floating through the air.
But I see tigers and mountains,
I know that they are there . . .
In the clouds.

Sam Du Rose (13)
Derby Independent Grammar School for Boys

DEATH THE SNIPER

Round the desolate earth
Speeds Death the Sniper.
All life dies
As he touches one and all.

All throughout the world
All creatures die and wither.
As he picks each man off
And destroys lives,
Using sorrow as a weapon.

Is it Death the Sniper
Who strikes the deadly blow
And drains all life?
Is it he who destroys
Joy and pain
And takes all life's pleasures away?

Daniel Gadsby (13)
Derby Independent Grammar School for Boys

THE CAT STRIKES

Silky fur of black.
Striding on your wall.
It's the cat!
Pounces on your garden wall.
You look at him.
He looks right back.
Before you know it.
He's on your flower bed.
A poor red rose.
Knocked down by its head.
The cat does a pose.
Then flicks some dirt.
Flies through the air.
Landing on a hanging shirt.
You start to scream and pull your hair.
The fluffy puss.
Makes an escape.
You'll get him next time.
Just wait and see . . .

Emily Sparrow (12)
High View School

THE DARK SHADOW

Slowly but surely it emerges from the wall.
It walks slowly down the hall.
I follow it trying not to be seen
If it sees me it might be mean.
It reaches out its hand to open the door.
But the door is locked.

Bang! Bang! It hits the wood.
I would've stopped it if I could.
The door flies open to reveal a charm.
I suddenly felt very calm.
I walked towards a bright light.
It jumped out and gave me a fright.
It was just my mother.
What a relief!
I though she was a thief.

Jennie Johnson (13)
High View School

LOVE LIFE

I was walking around
Safe and sound
Then I saw standing there
A beautiful girl with long brown hair
I tried so hard not to look
But she had me on her hook
Underneath those disco lights
She looked so innocent and nice
My friend went over, asked 'What's your name?'
Then she answered 'What's your game?'
I turned pretending not to know
That she was coming over to say 'Hello'
She said 'Hello,' I said 'Hi'
But I could not look her in the eye
I searched and searched for words to say . . .
Then she said 'Back in a mo, I'm going away'
Finally, I could breathe, I was sane
But I knew she'd be back again
I said to my mate 'What can I do?'
He said I'll ask her out for you
I shouted 'No' but it was too late
He'd gone to see that gorgeous girl's mate
When he came back I said 'You fool'
He said 'She's going to ask her for you'
Five minutes later she came over and said
'I like you'
I said 'That's great I like you too'
We went down and had a dance
I swear that I was in a trance
I looked her in the eye, and then to my surprise
We kissed. All my life I had waited for this.

Richard Vickers (14)
High View School

Untitled

A tree is big
As you can see
It's much bigger than you or me
It starts off small
And then it grows
The branches sway
As the wind blows
As the leaves fall off the trees
Then we know it's autumn.

Sian Barber (12)
High View School

MY LIFE IN HELL

My life in hell is hot and confused,
I wanted to tell you but the devil refused,
I rot and rot and wait to be set free,
But they say I have to wait an eternity,
'Let me go, let me go!' I shout and shout,
No one hears me, no one's about,
I have done no wrong, so let me go now,
I have done my punishment, but you say
you *don't know how.*

Helen Ireland (12)
High View School

BATS

Terrors in the darkness,
Squeaking in the wind.
Flapping round in circles,
Biting everything.

Hanging from the ceiling,
Like a string of coats.
How they're linked with vampires,
I would like to know.

In China bats are loved,
They show that peace is near.
So why do we dislike them,
When there's nothing to fear?

The reason for our hatred
Is what I want to know.
Why are we afraid of them?
Why do we hate them so?

Wayne Smith (14)
High View School

I'M AN ONION

I am an onion,
I am so strong,
I make people cry,
When I touch their tongue.

People leave me,
So I go brown,
When I wrinkle,
It looks like I frown.

To a salad or sandwich,
I give them a flavour,
I really do them a favour.

Carl Davis (13)
High View School

THE HOUSE!

The night is cold
The house is dark
The trees are blowing
And now it starts!

The ghouls and ghosts
Inside the house
Are crying out to scare the mice.

The spiders run
The bats hide
The ghostly figures go play and hide.

As daylight comes the house
Stands still
But still inside lies a ghostly chill.

Kirsty Rollett (13)
High View School

I AM A TREE

I am a tree
My leaves glide through the wind
In autumn my leaves fall
In different variations of colours
In winter I am bare
With no leaves on me.

I go cold while creatures hide within me
Hiding away from the cold wind and snow
In spring my leaves grow back
I warm up again and creatures stop hiding
They come out to smell
All the flowers which grow beside me
In summer I am very hot
But some days I am lucky
When the rain falls
I grow stronger.

Karl Slater (13)
High View School

THE CHEETAH

I am a cheetah
I clean myself to look great
My fur is so beautiful
The other animals admire me
I hunt all day
Trying to catch my very fast prey
When I run I am like lightning
To my prey I am very frightening.

Carl Day (13)
High View School

SAM

My dog Sam
He's got a golden tan
His eyes are soft and gentle, looking at me
His eyes are the same colour as the bark of the tree.

He runs against the wind
Crashing down on the grass as he goes
Chasing anything in sight that moves
After the running, Sam lies down and has a nap.

Twitching ears as he hears a cat outside
Sam jumps to his feet
For the cat he can't wait to meet
He runs to the back door
Barking to get my attention.

As soon as I let him out
He sniffs around
Then runs into the garden
About to give up
He sees the golden cat
Sam can catch it, the cat's fat.

Sam chases the cat
Through the grass
Jumping over some glass
Sam stumbles to the ground
The cat escapes
So Sam retires sadly back inside the house.

Louise Nightingale (14)
High View School

THE FIRE

As bright as the sun
As warm as an oven
As smelly as a welly
As noisy as a car
I spread in the woods
I spread in houses
I'm used to campfires
I'm used for cooking
Splash! Splash! Splash!
Then I die.

Ian Potter (12)
High View School

THE MANOR HOUSE

The manor house is dark,
The manor house is gloomy.
No one lives there but ghosts.
Cobwebs are everywhere,
The grass is black outside.
A solitary chair rocks on the porch.

The manor house is dark,
The manor house is gloomy.
Inside the hallway, pictures
Have eyes that stare and scare me.
Cracked shutters that flap in the wind,
Blowing the trees that look like ghosts.

The major house is dark,
The manor house is gloomy.
Old bones on the floor made my skin shiver
As I step by a few more steps
And I'm in the room
I'm glad to be home.

Charlotte Bancroft (12)
Landau Forte College

MOVING SCHOOL

The sweat keeps dripping,
The tears keep running,
The nightmare's coming,
It's getting closer and closer,
The day approaches,
Everyone's looking at you,
Hello, someone says,
And then you realise,
Starting a new school,
Isn't that bad after all.

Adelle McPhee (12)
Landau Forte College

DREAM

Quietly birds sing their happy song
In the distance a small cry from a baby owl
Wind slowly winding its way through the large leaves of a tropical tree
Sand slowly trickling through your bare toes
The soft splash of the sea in the distance
The perfect path winding slowly though the forest
Then a small cry of a small child in the distance
From a slow walk to a jog
The cry getting louder
From a jog to a run
Sprinting through the forest to help the poor child
Crying turning into a scream
Dream turning into a nightmare
Then a figure on a rock
A small child in a cot
Unattended and in pain
You pick the child up
The screaming stops
And then you wake up
Your dream over
Teddy bear in your arms
Mud all over your nightclothes.

Kristopher Vernon (11)
Landau Forte College

ACROSS THE ROOM

I sat across the room from her
Pretending to watch the grey skies
I'm pretty sure the whole class knew
I spent the whole lesson watching her eyes

I'd dream of her as I slept
At night I'd write sonnets in my head
As we passed in the halls
I'd guiltily think of her in my bed

Dreams should pass but this one wouldn't go
Even though I knew it for fantasy
I only watched, I never knew love
I don't even have the memories.

Krzysztof Wosik (14)
Landau Forte College

FREEDOM

We're trapped in a bubble with no way out,
how will we find what's without?
Only a few will ever work out
how to escape this bubble of life.
I could be free as a bird, but still stuck,
in this circular globe of life.
Freedom means I can go anywhere
but every time I'm stopped by our bubble.
Even with death we can never escape
as we are stuck by the constraints of our heaven or hell.
So can we ever be free?
Could we ever have complete freedom?
Will we ever know?

Christopher Manning (14)
Landau Forte College

THE TEACHER DISGUISE

I wonder what teachers are like
Underneath their teacher disguise.
I wonder if they ride a bike,
Or know how to hypnotise.

Do they go to parties
And get drunk on alcohol,
Or are they good at football
And always score a goal?

So under seventeens beware
And never trust a teacher,
Because you'll never know what teachers are like
Underneath their teacher disguise.

Puneet Bola (11)
Landau Forte College

GHOST HOUSE

G hostly groans, creaks and bangs
H ouse of darkness, cloaks and fangs
'O rrible ogres peeking through walls
S taring werewolf sits and calls
T he witch sitting on the stairs

H ouse of horrors, full of scares
O pen the door run out quick
U gly witch with magic stick
S hove the door open wide
E very breath feels good outside.

Maria McCabe (14)
Landau Forte College

CHILD SLAVERY

Here in 1830,
Still hard at work.
Our master Grimes is far too cruel,
He beats us and makes it hurt.
'Help us please!' He hears us plea,
It is as though he can't hear or see.
There are many other children
Treated just like this.
This is the one and only thing,
We really want to miss.

Here in the 1990s,
Still hard at work.
In other places this is so.
Many well-off people,
Just simply smirk.
Let's help make a change,
So the past is past,
And child slavery well out of range!

Deborah Hill (12)
Landau Forte College

SOMEONE SPECIAL

This is someone for who you care
Someone who will always be there

Someone who's been with you
Through thick and thin
Someone who's cheerful
Even when you're dim

Someone who's lots of fun
Someone to keep you on the run

Someone who will show they care
Someone who will be there.

Kelly Morgan (12)
Landau Forte College

I REMEMBER WHEN . . .

I remember when I was two
I flushed my mum's hanky down the loo!

I remember when I was three
I got stuck up in a tree!

I remember when I was four
I cut a hole in the door!

I remember when I was five
I taught my fish how to dive!

I remember when I was six
I got into an awful fix!

I remember when I was seven
I thought I was already in heaven!

I remember when I was eight
I fell off my garden gate!

I remember when I was nine
Everything I found was mine!

I remember when I was ten
I really wanted a pet hen!

And when I was eleven
I was really in seventh heaven!

Claire Southam (12)
Landau Forte College

WAR

Look at these men,
So strong, so brave,
If only they knew,
They'd be going to their grave.

Bombs dropping down everywhere,
Everyone knows the Germans don't care,
Always being told what to do,
This is the worst war, it's WW2.

All this anger, guilt, hate and pain,
I sincerely hope it'll never happen again,
Bombs, guns, anxiety, hope,
All the family at home have to cope.

As I look around me,
Just darkness do I see,
God, if I die now,
Will anyone find me?

Memories are all I have,
They're not for me to share,
Because I had to leave a friend,
Leave him dying there.

How many people,
Are going to die,
People said 'Fight for your country, slim chance of death,'
I've never heard such a lie.

Anastasia Hagan (13)
Landau Forte College

THE SILENT MURDER

In the darkness of the night he stalks his prey,
Monitoring each one from day to day.
He stalks the halls, suffocating every step,
This lonely midnight prowler, carries no regrets.
Watching, waiting in the shadows of darkness,
The ambitious predator, is slowly marching.
When the time has come, in one stealth like action,
The undetected, swooping vultures move in for satisfaction.

May it be the light of day, or the black of the night,
He carries one goal, one driving fight.
This tip-toeing psycho, of withering evil,
No pardon to give, no final reprieval.
Any man, any hunter, may soon be the hunted.
A stab to the back, or a shot to the head,
Either way you'll end up dead.
As the crackly voiced, adversary of the devil,
Does his job, he returns to hell.

Thomas Oakley (15)
Landau Forte College

COOPED UP IN A CAGE

Cooped up in a cage,
No one to talk to,
No one to know,
I wish they'd let me out of this
Small cramped cage.

What will they do to me next?
Test another line of make-up?
A different shampoo?
Don't they understand I need freedom too?

I sit all alone in my own little world,
My eyes stinging from the endless torture and hurt,
All I ask for is freedom,
Freedom to walk, freedom to be in my natural world.

The people they choose what they can do,
But me what can I say?
Cooped up in a cage,
No one to talk to,
No one to know,
Please let me have my freedom, let me out of this
Small cramped cage.

Emma Newstead (13)
Landau Forte College

MEMORIES

In a shrine of loneliness,
Surrounded by paper,
Reading over his words,
I've read too much . . .

His face still smiles,
In my mind words echo,
Yet his voice is silent.

Reading - always reading,
How do I touch him,
Love him, care for him?
I can't -
I've read too much . . .

One day becomes the next,
Every second the same,
As I blink, his eyes are within mine,
His touch upon my skin,
He becomes part of me,
Mine -
Every time.

Is this love?
Feeling lonely every day,
Memories painful to arise,
Memories - a graveyard of memories,
All that is left,
Of him and I.

Rebecca Gray (14)
Landau Forte College

HEROES AND VILLAINS

Wading through the trenches, thick and thin,
All was gloomy, the atmosphere dim,
As soon as we arrived we knew that we were doomed,
The end was drawing near me and Harold assumed,
The gunfire rattle, the devastating bombs,
Do we deserve to die? No we're not the ones,
What's the time? What's the day?
No one cares now you needn't say,
Every second tense, you might get hit!
Freezing in the trenches so dimly lit,
You can see in the clouds the birds, flying free,
If only I was there . . . I wish it was mine,
We'll just have to see, I may not return,
There's no winners just losers who serve the full-term.

Tesney Swann (14)
Landau Forte College

MY GARDEN

My very own patch of garden
Where everything is dead
My very own patch of garden
Wants flowers in its bed

My very own patch of garden
Is desperate to be hoed
My very own patch of garden
Can then be neatly sowed

My very own patch of garden
Wants blooms of pink and red
My very own patch of garden
Sits just next to the shed

My very own patch of garden
Has had so many seeds
I don't know where they go to
All I ever see in my garden is *weeds!*

Amy Spencer (11)
Landau Forte College

BEST FRIENDS

When best friends have an outing,
There are jolly times in store.
There are games and there are prizes,
There is also something more.

There's something in the hamper,
That's very good to eat,
When best friends have an outing,
It's a very special treat.

Holly Barlow (12)
Landau Forte College

THE BATTLE OF THE TRENCHES!

The darkness, the cold,
The smells and smoke of gunfire,
Drifting overhead,
Sitting waiting in the trenches,
For the enemy to try and shoot,
Us dead.

In the distance I could hear,
The screams of horror,
As blood is shed,
Sitting waiting in the trenches,
For them to arrive.

When the enemy reached our trenches,
Guns were fired,
Many dead,
Lots more dying all around me,
We fought the best we could!

We won *this* battle,
Of the trenches,
Lots of English and Germans dead,
So I waited,
For the next time,
To see if I would be among the dead!

Martin Simpson (13)
Landau Forte College

FREEDOM

The sound of war,
There's an open door,
It's the door to freedom,
But I can't reach it.

Bang, bang,
Another gun,
This is no fun,
My family in my mind.

Friends are far gone,
I'm now number one,
On the death list,
I need the door to freedom.

Why not peace?
This shouldn't be war,
We all need a door,
The door to freedom.

Jamie Birkin (11)
Landau Forte College

MY DOG FUSE

One day when I came home from school,
My mother had some bad news.
I could tell by the way she looked in my eyes,
It was to do with my dog Fuse.

She didn't have to say it,
I knew that something was up.
Please don't say he's dead,
Not my little pup.

Then she began to break the news,
How she'd taken him to the vet's.
He died at half past nine that day,
With lots of other pets.

A tear rolled down my face,
This was the end.
He wasn't just my dog,
He was my best friend.

Michael Siviter (12)
Landau Forte College

SIGNS AND SYMBOLS

Signs and symbols everywhere
Some are round,
Some are square,
Some say stop,
Some say go,
Some say cut down your speed and go slow,
Lollipop ladies,
Lollipop men,
Some signs you see again and again,
90 miles per hour is racing,
Signs are here for information.

Michelle Cain (11)
Landau Forte College

HOW SALLY FEELS

The birds twitter,
The frost glistens,
And small children dance and sing.
Sally shuffles her feet,
The frost bites her toes.
Salty tears sting her cheek,
But no one knows how Sally feels.

Smiling faces merge into school,
But Sally walks alone,
No friends,
No family,
No one.
Other children clap and laugh,
While Sally stares and prays.
She prays her life was like theirs,
But then, no one knows how Sally feels.

Loving arms from mums and dads fold around children's bodies,
Smiling faces, big bright eyes,
They tell the story of their day.
Sally has no one to tell,
No one to hug,
She's all alone.
No one can do anything because -
No one knows how Sally feels.

The birds twitter,
The frost glistens,
Small children dance and sing.
No one knows how Sally feels. Sally's all alone.

James Hassall (11)
Landau Forte College

THE MAN THAT GOT MAROONED

There was once a man that made a boat,
But he wasn't quite sure that it would float,
He tested it out on the sea one day,
But the wind blew him far, far away,
He landed on a desert island with tall palm trees,
And pine scented forests full of busy bees,
For seventy nights and seventy days,
He slept up a mountain, in a cave,
Then one day in early morn,
He heard the sound he'd been longing for,
Sitting in his cave in the light of dawn,
He heard the deep bellow of a ship's horn,
As the ship passed by he thought he was doomed,
But the crew finally noticed that he was marooned,
They picked him up, and he hitched a ride,
All the way back to the English seaside,
He looked out at the sea and looked rather glad,
He said 'I'm happy to be home but what an adventure I've had!'

Asim Rashid (11)
Landau Forte College

MY AUTISTIC BROTHER

My autistic brother,
Trouble is his game
Whenever things go crash and bang,
You'll always hear Dave's name.

He plays with dad's hi-fi
And when we tell him 'No,'
He will run away
As he's always on the go.

When eating his dinner,
He'll race from the table and watch telly,
He can't say my name properly,
So instead he calls me 'Jerry'.

He wrecks my cassettes on his Walkman,
But I think 'It doesn't really matter,
He's my special brother,
That's all that matters.'

Jenny Thorpe (11)
Landau Forte College

SENSE POETRY

Boredom
Looks like a museum
Sound like a silent film
Smells like damp air
Feels like dirty dust
Tastes like mushrooms on a damp day.

Surprise
Looks like presents under a Christmas tree
Sounds like fireworks going off
Smells like a stink bomb going off
Tastes like a birthday cake
Feels like paper as you unwrap your birthday presents.

Simon Inman (11)
Murray Park School

GALAXY!

I feverishly opened the wrapper, the smooth and mouth-watering
chocolate lay inside,
It was like a teddy waiting to be opened in a
parcel on Christmas day,
It looked like a small mud brick waiting to build a house,
The crunchy wrapper sounded like leaves under
your feet on an autumn day,
I put a piece of chocolatey brown chocolate towards
my mouth,
It tasted lovely, smooth and creamy like fresh milk
from a cow,
The chunky chocolate melted away in my mouth,
I was in paradise, it was Galaxy.

Kavita Rawal (12)
Murray Park School

THE PIED PIPER OF HAMELIN

It all took place in Brunswick,
Rats!
They ate the cheese out of the vats.
One day a piper went to call,
To see the mayor in his great hall.
I can get rid of them so don't dither,
With my pipe I'll drown them in a river.
No more rodents in the street,
Their lives end they soon would meet.
The piper went back,
Carrying for the guilders a sack.
The mayor said 'I'll make you a deal still rather nifty,
Come take fifty.'
The piper wouldn't stand for that,
He took the village children and never came back!

Sarah Lauder (11)
Murray Park School

HAPPINESS

Happiness looks like Manchester United winning,
Happiness sounds like Liverpool losing,
Happiness smells like fish and chips from Nicky's Fish Bar,
Happiness tastes like pizza from Deep Pan,
Happiness feels like a blanket wrapped round you on a cold day.

Hardeep Nanuwan (11)
Murray Park School

THE CREATURE THAT LURKS WITHIN THE TREES

Its eyes are like black pools of ink.
His teeth are like ivory daggers made
from elephants tusks.
The shape of his head is like a boulder
that has just fallen off a cliff.
A smell of mouldy cheese
passes my way every time it exhales.
There are gunshots and fireworks
sounds when one of those heavy, sharp
clawed feet makes contact with the ground.
Compared to his colossal body
his arms are like sharp ended knives.
Its skin is like a bed of crushed emeralds,
glistening in the sunlight.

Amber Collinge (11)
Murray Park School

LOVE

This is a letter from me to you,
just to say that I love you.
Lust and trust is all you need
to make a relationship work its need.

Our love has lasted every day,
because we love each other.
Our love is special in every way,
and it will last forever.

It started off as a hush,
then it started to a crush,
until we met face to face,
and decided to take it pace by pace.

I hope you read this letter,
just from me to you,
and just in case you didn't,
remember *I love you.*

Alison Blood (13)
Noel Baker Community School

BUS CRASHES WITH LORRY

Twenty-one people and nineteen children
Were injured in a bus *crash*
The lorry collided with the bus
And there was a might big *smash!*

The children were shouting and crying
So were the other people in the upper *deck*
The people had bruising and cuts
But the ambulance was soon there to *check.*

Some were taken to hospital
And the children's parents were told straight *away*
But no one was hurt seriously
And everything was soon *okay.*

Daniel Hamilton (12)
Noel Baker Community School

NIGHT IS . . .

Night is a time when all is asleep
Everyone's gone
But out in the darkness
There is a sound
A rustling of branches
A rustling of leaves
The night animals are coming out
Badgers and bats
Foxes and wolves
All creatures approaching quietly
But don't be afraid, they won't harm you
They're just out hunting for food.

Katy Heron (12)
Noel Baker Community School

ENGLAND

England play in blue and white,
the opposition get a fright.
David Seaman in the goal,
shouts 'Lads, we're on a roll.'
A cross from Beckham,
a header from Scholes
and the ball is in the goal!
Incey running down the wing,
hears the sound of a woodwork 'ding'
as Shearer's shot just missed by inches.
We couldn't believe it,
the keeper relieved,
as it spun right over the top.
England get a penalty as Campbell is brought down,
the keeper hardly believes it and so he gives a frown.
Owen steps up to take it,
he knows the keeper can't make it.
He scores,
the crowd roars,
and England triumph once again!

Alex Whyman (14)
Noel Baker Community School

ALIENS

Aliens are strange things,
Their heads look like balloons.
Their eyes are very big,
And their words sound like tunes.

They come down in spaceships,
And don't wear any clothes.
Their arms are long and bony,
And they only have two toes.

On the spaceship, there are funny lights,
They flash on and off.
They fly away, dust flies around
And that makes me cough!

Andrew Pell (14)
Noel Baker Community School

DIANA

She lead a beautiful life,
As our princess and our icon,
Such a precious life,
That you could not put a price on.

Until that horrific crash,
She helped the landmine campaign,
To stop all the landmines,
And to stop all the pain.

But on that night of the crash,
The 31st of August,
Diana did not know,
That her death would be so unjust.

The drunken driver drove,
At 100 miles per hour,
And as the car went out of control,
All his thoughts turned sour.

The car went screeching down the road,
A terrifying moment for all,
Then suddenly the car crashed,
Crashed into a brick wall.

The car stood still,
No longer going fast,
Inside Diana took a breath,
And that breath was her last.

Laura Wilkinson (13)
Noel Baker Community School

THE DINOSAUR

It was big, it was tall,
it could smash through a wall.
I ran and ran, but couldn't fall,
I looked behind and saw its face
and then it vanished without a trace.
I had to stop, I was out of breath,
I must admit I was scared to death.
Then my eyes opened, funny this may seem,
but I had just had a terrible dream.

Johnathan Bousfield (12)
Noel Baker Community School

LIFE

Teachers shout,
We all sneer,
Teachers shout,
We all have fear.

Lions roar,
Mice squeak,
Humans eat,
And have big feet.

Pens write,
Pencils draw,
People run,
Babies crawl.

Cars smoke,
People choke,
Bikes gleam,
Keep it clean.

Samantha Cooper (12)
Noel Baker Community School

THE WORLD!

The morning sky,
The morning dew,
The morning clouds,
The day is new.

The midday shower,
When we pass the hour,
And the clouds seem to fade away.

The evening knock,
As we strike twelve o'clock,
When the day has finally finished,
We find another's beginning.

Emma Hollis (14)
Noel Baker Community School

IN LOVE

I'm in love at first sight
With the boy down the street
I love him from his head
Right down to his feet

His lovely blonde hair
And his big blue eyes
Whenever I see him
I get hypnotised

I watch him in the day
And watch him in the night
When he walks left
I don't walk right
I put on my dress
And do up my shoes
When I get to school
I'll drag him in the loos

But stop! Look what's gone wrong?
He's standing with Katie
Has he been there for long?
They draw together,
I think he's in love, they kiss,
Oh no! I'll give her a shove.

I'm mad with the boy down the street
I'll punch him in his head and tread on his feet
With his straggly blond hair
And his ugly blue eyes

Now do you get the joke?
I'm good at telling lies.

Stacy Lowe (14)
Noel Baker Community School

ALIEN INVASION

Aliens from outer space
Beings from another race
Little green men who live on Mars
Driving around in supersonic cars
Coming down to invade our earth
To kill us all and destroy our birth
'We come in peace' at first they say
But it's too late anyway
We've made up our minds
We will attack
But the aliens will just fight back
With superior weapons unknown to man
They will defeat our measly clan
With just one shot the world goes bang
We have been beaten by the alien gang.

Liam Birch (14)
Noel Baker Community School

CLOUDS

The clouds are like butterflies,
floating all day long.

They're also like cotton wool balls,
drifting swiftly along.

The clouds are like patchwork quilts,
made up of different things.

The clouds look like paintings,
of very odd and peculiar things.

The clouds look like puffs of smoke,
moving in the air,
moving on so quickly,
that they always seem to disappear.

And I often wonder to myself,
what the world would be,
if there were no clouds in the sky,
would everything fall on me?

The clouds are like butterflies,
floating all day long.

They drift all day until one day,
maybe I'll wake up to find them all gone.

Charlotte Brown (13)
Noel Baker Community School

WHAT ARE GHOSTS REALLY LIKE?

Silvery white
Glistening in the light
Is that what ghosts are really like?

Slipping into shadows
Trying not to be seen
Are ghosts really mean?

Haunting people
Scaring them too
Is that what ghosts really do?

Maybe ghosts do exist
They are like a blurring mist
Scaring people they will persist
Perhaps ghosts really do exist.

Nicola Tabberer (13)
Noel Baker Community School

LOVE IS...

Love is a thing that can melt your heart
And make you go gooey inside
Make your knees wobble and tremble and shake
But love is a thing that can even break.

Love is the ring that you'll see on your finger
On the photos, the cake and the guests
But make sure this love is going to last
Then you will be in a perfect love nest.

Love is the family you'll soon want to start
With a child and its cheeky smile
Cherish these moments as great memories
That will live in your head all the while.

Love is the day Fourteenth of February
That will open your heart and soul
For your loved one will show you their love for you
With three words 'I love you'.

Love is a strong yet powerful thing
That will last if true and honest
To you and your precious loving one
You'll form a perfect love nest.

Nadene Usher (13)
Noel Baker Community School

THE BIG DAY

It's not a normal wedding
In fact it's all quite new
It won't be in a chapel
And the dress is different too.

It was held in Elvaston Castle
And the bride was wearing gold
She was wearing something blue and borrowed
Something new and old.

The cake was different flavours
The lemon was the best
After all had ate their piece
I nibbled at the rest.

Magicians and toasts in the afternoon
Dancing all the night
It seems that this fine day
Is turning out just right.

It's now the weekend after
And I'm remembering all the fun
While the couple are on their honeymoon
Relaxing in the sun.

Nicola Harris (13)
Noel Baker Community School

GHOSTS!

Do you believe in them, or do you not?
Most people believe you die and rot.
But I believe there are such things,
They float around as if with wings.
Are they normal, are they grey,
Are they unusual or just every day?
Do you believe in after death?
Have you experienced the unknown?
Have you ever seen a strange person?
Was it a ghost? Are you certain.
You're probably thinking you're not scared,
But I'll tell you, you will be.
If you see a ghost,
You just give it time,
You will see it with not a warning sign.

Haydn Bottrill (13)
Noel Baker Community School

FOOTBALL

In the yard at ten to nine,
In the yard at break,
On the field at dinner time,
Until our legs all ache.

Out there when it's cold and hard,
Out there in the rain,
That's the way with our lot:
Football on the brain.

Some like playing with yo-yos,
Some like games of chase,
Some just like to muck about,
And stand around the place.

But our lot run together,
With passes swift and neat,
Our lot's always on the move,
With a football at our feet.

Some say 'Why the trouble?'
Some say 'What's the fuss?'
But our lot's off to Wembley,
That's the place for us.
That's the way with our lot,
Football on the brain.

Paul Weldrick (14)
Noel Baker Community School

MY BIRTHDAY

On my birthday I awoke
As my sister sat up and spoke
'Happy Birthday, you're now 14
Eighty-six years you'll have a letter from the Queen.'

I walked downstairs with my sister behind
As I walked through the door what did I find?
There was my mum sitting with glee
And she opened her mouth and said
'Happy birthday' to me.

People coming all day long
Anyone would think there's something wrong
First my uncle, then my nan
Then my aunt who brought cousin Anne.

I opened my cards and said 'Thank you'
Everyone replied by saying
'Happy birthday to you!'

Sally Harte (14)
Noel Baker Community School

MY LIFE!

Born in 1984,
My mum was proud to be,
The mother of a baby,
That baby, it was me.

Everybody loved me,
They thought that I was great,
They kissed me and they held me,
That was until I was eight.

At eight, people called me a 'Bloomin' pest',
They told me what to do,
They made my life a living hell,
They ruled my life, it's true.

Now I'm fourteen, and it's still the same,
My parents rule my life,
I have no friends, no social life,
I have no love, no life!

I live each day,
The same as the others,
No difference, no change,
No bothers!

Lyndsay Harrison (14)
Noel Baker Community School

MY DRIFTING EMOTIONS!

I'm really full of hate,
Sometimes I think I'll cope!
I know how you really treat me,
So I'll just give up on hope!
Sometimes I want to comfort you
And keep you in my arms,
But now I just can see, we're falling right apart!

Is it you or is it me?
I simply just don't know,
But now I see we're drifting,
Much like life I just know!

Lisa James (14)
Noel Baker Community School

ONE MEMORY

The new shiny leaves and
The old ones too,
To touch with my hand
Under the clear skies of blue.

I remember when the poor thing
Had just been a seed,
And with it I planted my fake silver ring
Hoping to grow more rings which I did need.

Granny had laughed
And said I was daft,
She told my mum,
Who said 'What have you done?'

I got so scared
And ran to the tree,
And I found my ring
That was good for me.

Well now the tree is fully grown,
And I am not going to moan.

Rebecca McIntyre (13)
Noel Baker Community School

SUMMER

Summer is a time for happiness
When all is bright and precipitation is out of sight
Summer is a time of sun
When birds tweet and people have fun
Summer is the time for sunloungers
And the growth of pretty flowers
Summer is the time of year
When I come out of hibernation
Summer is the time of year
That my family and I go on vacation.

Carly Grimadell (13)
Noel Baker Community School

IN EACH SEASON

Go into the forest in the spring
When the world feels fresh and new
When birds appear, green sprigs grow
And the new grown grass is sparkling
Speckled with morning's dew.

Go into the forest in the summer
When the sun's rays dart between trees
When all the plants and flowers are in full bloom
And the secretive song of the bird
Is carried away by a soft summer breeze.

Go into the forest in the autumn
When things are dull and dry
When all the animals hide away
From the approaching cold
Down in a warm hole or in the trees way up high.

Go into the forest in the winter
When the air is silent and still
When the only noise is the patter of rain
But soon the spring will be here again
And the silence will be broken!

Lara Whitmore (13)
Noel Baker Community School

DOGS

Afghans, Labradors - very tame.
Collies, sheepdogs - about the same.
Pit-bulls can be large or small
Great Danes are always very tall.

Alsations a great dog to keep.
Whippets are always asleep.
Airedales are always last.
Yorkshire Terriers are extremely fast.

Shih-tzu nippy but tiny
Bull terriers are always whining.
Dobermans are brilliantly streamlined.
Dogs for the blind - are very kind.

Terriers are killers.
Dalmations are spotty
Poodles are fluffy
And Jack Russell's are dotty.

Daniel Lyth (12)
Noel Baker Community School

TITANIC

Today is the start of my voyage
I'm sailing across the seas.
Before I reach the end
I hope to meet the man of my dreams.

How could I tell him how I felt
I turned the corner and there he stood.
Towards him I walked along the deck
Shall I tell him, I don't know if I could.

We were together in each others arms
It was love at first sight.
Something was happening all around
All I could see was a flashing light.

There was panic all over the ship.
I felt it tilting to the side.
I looked for my lover, I couldn't find
All I wanted to do was hide.

I looked everywhere
I heard my lover scream.
We tried to get on a rescue boat
But rich people were all they'd seen.

I did have a dream
All I wanted was to be his wife.
But it was taken away from me
Because to save me - he gave up his life.

Becky Grace (12)
Noel Baker Community School

THE SECRET OF POMPEII

Walking all round the city streets,
selling, talking and trading.
They didn't know what was to come
in Vesuvius waiting.

An almighty bang filled the air,
and everyone turned to see.
A billowing cloud of black smoke,
was nearing so rapidly.

So they quickly dived for cover
in every possible place.
But alas nothing could save them,
from the fate they were to face.

Women tried to save their children,
dogs protected their masters.
But despite their desperate efforts
it ended in disaster.

Cocooning them in sheaths of ash,
imprinting their last actions.
The city now frozen in time,
capturing their reactions.

And then one day they were all found,
just like statues made of stone.
The secret of Pompeii was out,
but names are still left unknown.

Hannah Murton (13)
Noel Baker Community School

ERIC THE SPITTER

Eric the spitter could spit quite far
He spat over the top of a Jaguar.
The people who saw him called him spitfire
but he can also be a very big liar.

He lied about spitting on the teacher's chair
He lied about spitting in the teacher's hair
He also got all the words wrong.

But Eric is gone, too soon alas
He will also be missed by his class.
The school was shut for the day
To see their friend go away.

Ian Furnival (12)
Noel Baker Community School

TITANIC

Titanic was built with so much pride
Nobody knew that it would be their last ride.
But friends were formed and love knew no bounds.
They said it would never sink but somebody lied.

The party was in full flow.
Nobody knew of the danger.
Maybe that was a blessing we will never know.
Friends became no longer strangers.

But the deepest tragedy of it all
Was for the two lovers that had yet to fall.
Their eyes had met but their lips haven't touched
They had just danced together at the ship's ball.

And finally when they came together,
Their hearts gleamed with passionate desire.
And together they danced and are dancing still.
Next to them was a blazing fire.

When out of the blue they struck some ice
They shouted and screamed in despair.
But the Atlantic ocean was so cold.
The Titanic wreck lies somewhere down there.

Lisa Lomax (12)
Noel Baker Community School

DIANA'S BALLAD

Down in France at midnight
A car sped down the highway.
With the paparazzi right behind them
Faster they went all the way.

Going faster and faster
They skidded round the bend.
The tunnel came upon them
It seemed never to end.

The car raced, raced
The tunnel became evil.
The car kept going faster
They thought they saw the devil.

He laughed at them
When the crash happened.
Diana, Dodi and the driver died
Slowly the message was spread.

David Hambling (12)
Noel Baker Community School

DIANA'S DEATH

Diana's death was tragic
in every way.
I'm sure her sons William and Harry
would have wanted her to stay.

On that morning when people heard the news
of the car crash in Paris.
Her two sons that she adored
didn't even get a last kiss.

Everybody was sad
and everyone mourned her death.
While her sons tried to hold their heads up
when they were really depressed.

She did a lot of charity work
and helped try to stop land-mines.
She visited people in hospital
and tried to save some lives.

She visited poor countries
and loved to see,
people who got better
that made her happy.

Donna Johnson (13)
Noel Baker Community School

TITANIC

As the sea is calm
The moon is full bright.
Titanic is on its way through the calm waters.

Away it goes quiet and gentle
The moon is still full bright.
As it goes through the sea.
The bright light shines onto the water.

The journey is fine.
As it travels there's no hint of a disaster.
People are calm and happy.

Suddenly the Titanic hits an iceberg
It drowns the beautiful and only bright light,
Plus our own Titanic too.

The world is sad, Titanic is gone they say,
But is there any hope of it coming back?
But no sound or news
The Titanic has really gone.

As the people weep.
They say we not only think of the Titanic as a ship
But it was in our hearts.

As they say the Titanic was a special friend.
But the sadness has not gone.
And still today people miss the Titanic.

Shahriza Naz Ali (12)
Noel Baker Community School

A POEM

I've got to write a poem
but where do I begin?
I've got to find words that rhyme
and try to fit them in.

What do you think I should write about?
Oh! Please give me a clue.
All these words in my mind.
I don't know what to do.

I need to start at the beginning
not forgetting the middle or the end.
So many things I try to say
it's driving me round the bend.

Peace has come to me
now my mind is clear.
All these words now I'm able to see
my pen is in fifth gear.

I hand it in I'm given the all clear
Help me please!
I'm going to faint with fear
I look up not a word - just a smile.

Joelle Italici (12)
Noel Baker Community School

INTO THE WOODS . . .

Into these ancient, moss-filled glades
I decided to take off my rollerblades.
I couldn't walk on these broken twigs
Before me I saw a herd of pigs.
Rotten fruit they gobbled up.
The earth beneath them all churned up.
Away they ran into the trees
'Oh God!' I cry 'here come the bees!'
Buzzing around as they form their attack.
Oh, that's it! I'm going back.
Back to the sunshine and open fields.
I'm getting mobile, back on my wheels.

Joanna Jenkinson (12)
Noel Baker Community School

THE BALLAD OF DIANA

Diana! Diana! Diana!
She was a strong wilful lady
Who thought nothing of helping anyone
May it be a mother, father or a baby.

Wind, rain or fall
Diana would come out
to hear young children talk to her
whisper, scream or shout.

But then one night, one fateful night
'twas Diana's turn to shout.
'Slow down quickly!' she cried
'Paul Henri - look out!'

Then there was a piercing scream
an awful shattering noise
and as Diana lay there suffering
her thoughts were of her boys.

William and Harry were their names
the heir and spare to be.
But surviving the awful crash that night
Diana was not to see.

The whole world awakes
and the whole world starts
to sense the loss that we all felt
for our tragic Queen of Hearts.

The funeral came, the funeral went
in a black car she lay.
Flowers were thrown in the air
as were a mix of feelings that day.

Whether you loved her or loathed her
you can surely see.
The pain that's left within us
is as it will always be.

Goodbye English Rose . . .

Claire Louise Richardson (12)
Noel Baker Community School

BIG TOP BEAR

Muzzled and on a leash
Fred the Canadian bear
Trapped in a cage
Nobody has a care.

Fred performs in a circus
Instead of roaming in a wood
Eating stale cakes and wilted carrots
Fred dreams he is in a wood - he wishes he could.

Fred is five years old
But he looks more.
Fred's owners say they care
But I bet they think Fred's a bore.

Fred's maybe going to be put down
His owners don't care.
Fred's done nothing wrong.
Fred's a poor little bear.

Gemma Marsh (12)
Noel Baker Community School

PRINCESS DIANA

There once was a loving princess
Diana was her name
As everyone lives and dies
Well one day - hers just came.

She cared for almost everyone
But all that had to end.
She could be close to anyone
A very special friend.

She'll be in our minds forever
For all the years and years.
But everyone will carry on
Trying to hide those tears.

Kirsty Caple (12)
Noel Baker Community School

DIANA

That beautiful face
wasted away.
Leaving the nation
in sorrow for more than a day.

She's been gone for
more than a year
but still we shed
that lonely tear.

In our hearts she'll
always be here
but still we try to
hold back that lonely tear.

Helping others is what
she lived for
but now everyone is
feeling so sore.

Her sons try to
hold back that lonely tear
but in their hearts
they have missed her all year.

Her lips as red as roses
her eyes beautiful everyday
in our eyes she's with us
in each and every way.

She found her love in Dodi
but the papers wouldn't go
away on the night she
went they took her love away.

Kirsty Dolman (12)
Noel Baker Community School

TRICK OR TREAT

Hallowe'en is an exciting night
Although one of the coldest in the year.
It may be raining, but we don't care
Still we dress up in horrible gear.

Some kids pretend to be Dracula
Happy trampling around in the mud.
Wearing long black cloaks and sharp-looking fangs
They have mouths that are covered with blood.

The girls love to dress up as witches,
On their heads they wear long pointed hats.
They cast spells on all of their neighbours,
On broomsticks they have their black cats.

Kids wearing costumes, knock at the doors
Everyone shouts 'Trick or treat?'
Some may end up with a joke
But most go home with a sweet.

Ghosties and ghoulies and black hairy beasties
Which all go bump in the night.
They are the things that I like best
But seem to give people a fright

Phillip Moore (12)
Noel Baker Community School

THE GUNPOWDER PLOT

In the 17th Century, Guy Fawkes was alive
he had a nasty devious mind.
I think Guy Fawkes was a bit strange
he plotted a lot, you might find.

Guy Fawkes you see had a lot of connections
with horrible men who weren't tame.
They were going to blow up the Houses of Parliament
as you see they were insane.

With kegs of gunpowder all tied up
into the houses they all snuck.
They were determined not to get caught
but they had no such luck.

The guards caught them in the act,
arrested and tried in front of the crowd.
They were sentenced to death,
the cheers of glory were loud.

With a velvet rope around his neck
there he was hung, drawn and quartered.
His head on the end of a fork
now you can see he was thoroughly slaughtered.

We all put him on our bonfires
and sit in the street saying 'Penny for the guy.'
We let him burn again and again
His memory will never die.

Emma Veldeman (13)
Noel Baker Community School

THE END OF THE ROAD!

Two little animals sittin' in the road.
One was a hedgehog, one was a toad.
Along came a lorry with a load.
Squashed the little hedgehog, squashed the little toad.
Away to heaven hedgehog, away to heaven toad
Away went the lorry - down the road.

Claire Simmons (12)
Noel Baker Community School

CHRISTOPHER COLUMBUS

In fourteen hundred and ninety two
Three ships tied by the quay.
Were off to sail the ocean blue
And soon put out to sea.

The captain was Columbus
The crew were all afraid.
To India for spices
With goods on board to trade.

Through stormy seas and winds
Far west through day and night.
Columbus saw a wonderful view
As land came into sight.

The crew all cheered 'It's India!'
But although this was not true.
Columbus called them the West Indies
These islands are fair and fine and new.

Ellena Knott (13)
Noel Baker Community School

TOMMY POWELL

Tommy Powell a hero
Guiding Derby through the fight.
He made the crowd so proud
Giving the away fans such a fright.

406 appearances for the team
Making Derby fans roar with might.
Showing some discipline
In the black and the white.

The BBG was the place
To see Tommy Powell win the race.
To score lots of goals
With his tremendous pace.

A well-loved man, a legend of time
He was a footballer's hero
And a family man,
May there be love and respect
Always to show.

Samantha Hibbert (12)
Noel Baker Community School

AN ANIMALS' HOME

Animals, animals everywhere.
Lions, tigers, they don't care.
In the wild roaming free
Having zebra for lunch or tea.

Animals, animals everywhere.
Hamsters, gerbils they don't care.
Trapped in a cage, snoozing, sleeping
Depending on you for their keeping.

Animals, animals everywhere.
Monkeys, gorillas they don't care.
In an area with public viewing
Children pointing, staring, booing.

Animals, animals everywhere.
Elephants, sea lions, they don't care.
Slowly parading around the ring
Always expected to fetch and bring.

Animals, animals everywhere . . .

Timothy Oxley (12)
Noel Baker Community School

THE BLACK DEATH

The Black Death was coming
it was coming towards us.
Spread by rats and fleas
and coughs and sneezes.

The doors were marked with crosses
to let people know the disease was there.
The bodies were taken in carts,
put in piles and burnt
the black smoke filled the air.

When they caught the disease
some of them coughed up blood.
And had big black blisters,
and listed them no good.

You wouldn't have guessed that the Black Death
is still going on now.
Several hundred people still catch the disease,
but people can't think how!

Christy Maritz (12)
Noel Baker Community School

NOVEMBER 5TH

The day on which a man was found
trying to commit an act of treason.
We celebrate by lighting bonfires
and burning dummies on top of them.

We buy some fireworks
then set them off.
A million different
all lighting up the sky.

A rocket goes up
then explodes in mid-air.
Some Catherine Wheels
with their colours so bright.

Then up go the bangers
they only go low.
But what a big bang.
Boy! What a show!

The evening ends
with hot dogs and potatoes
and everybody
sitting round the bonfire.

Adam Buxton (12)
Noel Baker Community School

IN THE INFANTS

In the Infants at playtime
The teachers hide away.
To save themselves from riots,
While keeping warm on a cold day.

The children stand and huddle,
Their fingers turning blue.
It's cold and they are freezing,
They can't even go to the loo!

Annie's been sick in the corner,
Alfie walked into a tree!
Charlotte has bumped into Hannah,
And John has hurt his knee.

The children stand still on the whistle,
Keep quiet like little gnomes.
It will soon be time for dinner,
Afternoon, then time to go home.

They went in nice and quietly,
But Alice was making a noise.
Jamie was being a nuisance,
Claire was playing with her toys.

The teachers come out of the staffroom
With biscuits and cups of tea,
To munch at during the lesson.
The teacher's the one to be!

Emma Whyman (12)
Noel Baker Community School

MY FAMILY

My mother's name is Sandra,
Hilda's her middle name.
She finally divorced my father Bob,
after playing second best to a footy game.

Susie, that's my sister,
has hair to match her ginger cat.
Bobby, he's my brother,
won't put down his baseball bat.

Gracie, my youngest cousin,
owns Barbie sets galore.
Harry, my other cousin,
eats chocolates by the score.

My Uncle Simon and Auntie Bett
love all films black and white.
My Auntie Pat loves wrestling,
shouting 'I'll give you a fight!'

My Grandma loves Eastenders,
she's never missed one yet.
My Grandad snores away the hours
when he's not down the bookies placing a bet.

Now you've met my family,
I had better go.
Before I start on about myself,
with things you really wouldn't like to know.

Natalie Lorraine Garton (12)
Noel Baker Community School

MUNICH!

They were flying over Munich
and the score had been 3 - 3.
They were all a bit upset
maybe the pilot couldn't see!

It might have been the weather
If only they had left later.
The ones who died might have survived
their chances would have been greater.

Why? How? Were the questions going round.
The whole of the country was in mourning.
The poor women who were now widows
Also thinking of their husbands who had
died that morning.

Now the manager had troubles.
He didn't have a team.
He never thought this would happen
not even in his wildest dreams.

A bleak day in football history
8 died
A fine team it was
5 survived . . .

Samara Dar (12)
Noel Baker Community School

WHAT LOVE REALLY MEANS?

Real love is stronger than anything in the world,
It's much more than an expensive, precious pearl.
If you're not careful, it might take you by surprise,
It may break your heart and make you cry.

Kisses so sweet and tender,
His smile, you will always remember.
When he hugs you with his loving arms,
The tips of his fingers give out his special charms.

I love him more than words can say,
I think about him every day.
Through my life, I want him to be there,
Without him, my heart will feel bare.

Natalie Mellor (12)
Noel Baker Community School

TELEVISION

TV my favourite past time,
I like watching it anytime.
Remote control by my side,
On the other TV guide.

Sister Sister on Nickelodeon,
Twins, Tamera and Tia.
Their family gives them lots of attention,
I wish I had that sort of career.

Sky One, I watch The Simpsons,
Maggie, Lisa, Bart, Marge and Homer.
Bart, Lisa and Maggie have bundles of fun,
Marge makes me laugh and Homer's a moaner.

BBC 1, the one to view,
If you like Top of the Pops.
B*witched, Backstreet Boys, U2,
The same as what you get on the box.

Sky One, Channel 5, BBC, ITV,
It's doesn't matter to me as long as it's TV.
Bart Simpson, Tia, Tamera, Spice Girls, Kylie,
It doesn't matter to me as long as it's TV.

Keighley Flynn (12)
Noel Baker Community School

HENRY THE VIII

Henry the VIII was a Royal boar,
He always had to start a war,
The worst excuse he had of all,
'I had to, it's English law.'

Henry the VIII was extremely cruel,
He fed the peasants revolting gruel,
And even when his heart went soft,
He was as stubborn as a mule.

Henry the VIII had VI wives,
Altogether his VI wives had VI lives,
And when his wives were killed, well,
There must have been VI blood stained knives.

Daniel Hilliard (12)
Noel Baker Community School

DISNEYLAND PARIS

If I could think of one place
I'd really like to go,
It would have to be Disneyland
In Paris, France you know.

I'd set off very early and I'd really
Hope it doesn't rain,
I'd travel through the tunnel on
The Shuttle train.

I'd love my photo taken with
Donald Duck and Mickey Mouse,
Then I'd ride the scary Black Hole,
And visit the Haunted House.

I'd go to see the Grand parade
Because all my favourite characters would be there,
Then all night there'd be the fireworks
Rockets flashing in the air.

The day is nearly over and it is
Time to go home,
Back to England and to school
Never more to roam!

Laura Hazell (12)
Noel Baker Community School

Is Silence Golden?

Is silence really golden?
I will never know
I'm surrounded by silence
Everywhere I go

Through my eyes I see
The world that waits out there
Beyond my silent world
Is a lion's lair

In a world so big
And frightening as well
I'd like to hear a bird
Or a chiming bell

Looking now around me
I wonder at the sounds
This world is creating
As it slowly turns around

There are others like me
Cocooned within this shell
Is silence golden?
We cannot tell

I talk with my hands
And listen with my eyes
So, silence is golden?
Maybe it's all lies.

Jennifer Miller (14)
Royal School for the Deaf

THE FOOTBALL

I like football
Sometimes I get wet
I go on the grass when it's muddy
To see how dirty I can get.

My poor mum was in tears
When she saw me at the door
She says if I keep on getting muddy
I can't play football any more.

Katie Lane (14)
Sinfin Community School

THE NIGHT WHEN THE WIND CAME

My heart was pounding,
As the wind was sounding,
On one late November's night.

I was gonna turn away but I had
To see the wind to feel the light,
Then I socialised in the river's mountain
Which was designed for you.

One minute was so long but you
Were there to save me,
We were standing there in the
Dark . . . last night.

Pardeep Lidhar (13)
Sinfin Community School

SPRING

Red rose petals, dark green leaves,
Beautiful butterflies, fly above me.
    Spring is coming.

Freshly cut grass, beneath the apple trees,
Green, green meadows with horses running free.
    Spring is near.

Birds singing high up in the trees,
Rabbits running across the mellow greens.
    Spring is finally here.

Inderjeet Chera (14)
Sinfin Community School

MY CAT TIGER

(Shortly after I wrote this poem about my cat, he was hit by a car and died. I woud like to dedicate this poem to his memory, he was only five months old)

T is the window sill, his favourite place
I is for an invitingly friendly, but cute little face
G is for when he greets me with a miaow every day
E is for eagerly wanting to jump and play
R is for resting by the fire at the end of the day.

Nikkita Dyche (11)
Sinfin Community School

A YOUNG ANORAK'S OPINION

Poor old Richard Branson,
    He has got it wrong,
    He bought the West Coast Mainline
    When going for a song.

His airline runs to schedule,
    Without customer complaint,
    But getting trains to run on time,
    Is something which he aint.

He shifts the blame to Railtrack,
    And this is only fair.
    He know his trains would run on time,
    If Railtrack took more care.

If I had a magic wand,
    I'd wave it in his direction,
    Then I'd gladly catch his trains,
    To reach my destination.

Richard Timmins (11)
Sinfin Community School

THE STORM

I look out of my window,
The clouds are turning grey,
Thunder booms like big brass drums,
Rain falls like big buckets of water,
Being thrown all over town.

I sit and watch with amazement,
As next door's cat runs for shelter,
As lightning bolts across the sky,
Like a flash of neon light,
And as the rain falls faster and faster.

And then the rain begins to stop,
And the clouds begin to float away,
The sky is blue and clear,
And the air smells of wet soil.

Then people down the street,
Emerge from their houses,
To see the damage that is done,
By the dangerous, almighty *storm*.

Marsha Davidson (13)
Sinfin Community School

FOOD

Eggs, bacon, cheese and ham
Cook them in the frying pan
When they're sweet, they're ready to eat
Give the egg a real good beat.

Zoe Keeling (12)
Sinfin Community School

THINKING ABOUT . . .

I've been asked to write a poem today,
I've been trying to think of what to say.
Could I write about this or that,
Or should I write about next door's cat?

I'm sitting here looking around,
Oh look, I've just found a pound.
I think I'll go and spend this money,
I might even think of something funny.

I stand there wondering what to buy,
I give my money to the man in the tie.
Opening the wrapper is such a struggle,
Someone knocks into me and it flies into a puddle!

Wet and soggy I fish it out,
It's not this much bother fishing for trout.
I've been asked to write a poem today,
I think I'll leave it for another day!

Chris Tite (13)
Sinfin Community School

THE WIND

Who has seen the wind?
Neither I or you,
But when the leaves are trembling
The wind is passing through.

Who has seen the wind?
Neither you or I,
But when the trees bow down their heads,
The wind is passing by.

Jamie Varnham (11)
Sinfin Community School

THE GHOST

I walked through the woods,
Footsteps were following me,
I turned around,
There is nothing there.

I feel something on my back,
There's a track,
I start to run,
Something in the woods is having fun.

It scares me,
Something is out there,
I feel a hand on my hair,
I feel dead scared now.

I think it's a ghost,
So be aware,
There's a ghost over there,
Help, he's got me!

Faye Hambleton (12)
Sinfin Community School

SPACE AS I SEE IT!

In space the sun burns like a
ball of fire.
In space the planets move like
the balls on a snooker table.
In space the stars shine like the
smiles on our faces.
In space the black holes open
and swallow like a hippo yawning.
In space the comets fly like kites
in the sky with their tails behind them.
In space the earth is like an
amoeba in the biggest ocean.

Sarah Todd (13)
Sinfin Community School

THE HOLE MONSTER

Oh monster, oh monster,
You're not going to fool me.
I can see this hole so clear.
I am not going to fall like a sack of potatoes
In the deep, deep hole.

Oh monster, oh monster,
I am not that thick -
I have eyes and ears,
And socks and knicks.
So I am not going to fall,
Down this . . . er . . . deep . . . deeep hooooole!

'Ha, ha, ha, he, has human headache,
Ha, ha, hoooooo!'
Buff! Bang! 'Oh blast. Oh God help!'
Buff, bang, crack!

Silence in the hill came,
With only noises from the cave,
And all you can hear is *buff* and *bang,*
And the monster making boys as slaves.

Emma Yeomans (13)
Sinfin Community School

I'D LOVE TO BE . . .

I'd love to be a boat,
To sail the world and float,
And go past all the country's as a lovely boat,
But I'd rather be the moon.

I'd love to be the moon,
Shining bright all through the night,
And lighting up the sky,
But I'd rather be an astronaut.

I'd love to be an astronaut,
To walk around in space,
And listen to my favourite music which is
Sung by Mase.
But I'd rather just be me.

Sonia Bassi (14)
Sinfin Community School

FREEDOM

F reedom to me is an open space
R epresenting freedom is a dove
E verywhere a dove can go
E verywhere a dove can fly
D oing anything you want to do
O verflowing happiness
M y bird of freedom.

Stephanie Robinson (12)
Sinfin Community School

FREEDOM

Freedom means to be free,
Free to be what you want when you want,
Free to run around,
Freedom means to be out in the open.

Freedom means to be free,
Free to have a say,
Free to have rights,
Freedom means to run along a sandy beach.

Freedom means to be free,
No one to boss you around,
Free to see who you want, when you want,
No curfews, no rules, no contracts.

Freedom means to say what you feel,
Or what you think,
Freedom means to be free like a bird,
To fly in the sky, through the clouds.

Freedom to me means to be free.

Hayley Stower (12)
Sinfin Community School

A WORLD OF FANTASY

Dragons and unicorns,
Werewolves and witches,
Live in our dreams,
In a world of fantasy.

Dragons breathing fire,
Large teeth and jagged claws,
A nightmare in our dreams,
In a world of fantasy.

Unicorns so majestic,
Horn glittering in the sun,
Magic in our dreams,
In a world of fantasy.

Werewolves and witches,
Giants and trolls,
A nightmare in our dreams,
In a world of fantasy.

Nightmares and dreams,
Dragons and unicorns,
We can think of anything,
From the world of fantasy.

Lindsay Rawson (12)
Sinfin Community School

FREEDOM

(This poem is about when Africa was owned by white people,
there has been no racism since 1981.)

F reedom which involves me
R oads to a happy place
E ducation with real meaning
E ntrances for black people as well
D anger which has no part of me
O ver a happy green land
M y happy land, will it be free . . .

Sukbinder Bains (12)
Sinfin Community School

FREEDOM

F reedom means to be free
R acism stopped
E verybody's free
E veryone's happy
D ove of Peace
O ver a happy green land
M ove peace throughout the world.

Christopher Storry (12)
Sinfin Community School

BLACK

B lack is the colour of night and then the
L amp lights go bright
A nd black is also the colour of a killer whale
C ircling around you when you're gone for a swim
K ing of the killer whales is heading for you.

Laura Lakin (12)
Sinfin Community School

BLACK

Black is the colour of dark
Dark black is the colour of a tunnel
Black is the colour of rats
Black rats running through the dark black kitchen
Black is the colour of navy black
Navy black is the colour of my socks
Black is the colour of black shoes
Black shoes which I wear to school
Black is the colour of jail bars
Jail bars which lock you in
Black is the colour of cows
Black cows eating grass.

Joti Atwal (11)
Sinfin Community School

GOODBYE

Goodbye is a word we
all could not say
for the birds were humming
for they didn't have to say
it today
For everyone knows forever
friends don't part but today
they do but not in their
loving hearts.

Mandeep Dhillon (11)
Sinfin Community School

MY FAMILY

My mum is fat,
My dad is weak,
We have a cat,
We have a bird
With a beak.

(Now to talk about my mum.)

Every Monday my mum went shopping,
She shopped till she dropped
Wishing from good to bad
She made the money go pop.

(Now to talk about my dad.)

Every Monday my dad cleaned the house,
Every time he found a mouse,
Wishing from good to bad,
He kicked them out the house.

My mum is nice,
My dad is kind,
We have mice
We know that he
Doesn't mind.

Roshni Karia (11)
Sinfin Community School

RED

Red is the colour of blood that runs down when you fall.
Red is the colour of roses, tulips, poppies and carnations.
Red is the colour of juicy strawberries which make your mouth water.
Red is the colour of Asian and Chinese wedding dresses.
Red is the colour of autumn leaves falling off the trees.
It is the colour of apples and red wine.
Red is the colour of head lice walking around in some people's hair.
When I think of red I think of a hot day.
Red also reminds me of a vibrant atmosphere.

Satinder Dhamrait (11)
Sinfin Community School

TWINKLE TWINKLE

Twinkle twinkle chocolate bar
My dad drives a rusty car
Push the starter, pulls the smoke
When my grandma's vases broke.

Danwell Francis (11)
Sinfin Community School

FOOTBALLERS

Why do girls like footballers?
All they do is sweat.
They smell of old muddy socks,
And they get all dirty and wet.

Girls like Michael Owen,
They think he is nice and cute.
My thought on the situation is,
They make me want to puke.

Football is a good sport,
Except the players don't follow the rules.
They are the ugliest people in the world,
They're all a crowd of fools.

All they do is sleep all day,
They don't do any work.
They go down to the pub every day,
They're all a bunch of jerks.

Wayne Cross (11)
Sinfin Community School

CHILDREN

Children, children
Yes mother
Where have you been?
To see papa
What did you eat?
Bread and cheese
Where is my share?
Up in the air
How will I get it?
Stand on a chair
What if I fall?
I don't care
Get my share
From the air
Make it, bake it
With some care.

Carrie Reeves (11)
Sinfin Community School

RED

Red is the colour of my clothes,
Red is the colour of my sister's favourite colour,
Red is the colour of my writing,
Red is the colour of my pen,
Red is the colour of a chilli,
Red is the colour of a strawberry,
Red is the colour of a cherry,
Red is the colour of a drink,
Red is the colour of Mars,
Red is the colour of a rose,
Red is the colour on my mind,
Red is the colour in my heart,
Red is the colour of love,
Red is the colour of my heart,
Red is the colour of my blood,
Red is the colour of death.

Kayleigh Cobley (11)
Sinfin Community School

MY PLAYSTATION

My PlayStation is really cool,
If you try to stop me you're a fool.
Don't try to stop me because if you do,
I will well and truly kill you.

My PlayStation is the best,
It is better than all of the rest.
My mum wants a go,
I just sit there and say 'So.'

My PlayStation is really neat,
It is way, way better than a compost heap.
My mum tries to bribe me away,
I just sit there and start to play.

Daniel Scott & Scott Thompson (11)
Sinfin Community School

A DARK COLOUR BLACK

Black is the colour of death
Black is the colour of sadness
Black is the colour of night
Black is the colour of the Black Sea
Black is the colour of the blackboards
Black is the colour of the Dead Sea
Black is the colour of black paper
Black is the colour of blackbirds
Black is the colour of coal
Black is the colour of tar
Black is the colour of black cats
Black is the colour of panthers
Black is the colour of my pen
Black is the colour of Black Jacks
Black is the colour of dogs
Black is the colour of shoe polish
Black is the colour of ants
Black is the colour of black eyes
Black is the colour of T-shirts
Black is the colour of your pupil.

Sian Barber (11)
Sinfin Community School

A POEM ABOUT LIVERPOOL

I stand in the Liverpool stand
Because I'm a Liverpool fan
Liverpool are the best
Because we can beat all the rest
Forget the Arsenal and Man U
Liverpool are the club to view.

Jagdeep Chohan (11)
Sinfin Community School

WINTER

Cold and chilly, morning and noon
Snow on the ground, low bright moon
Birds flying south where the sun always shines
Men in the pubs drinking brandy and wines

Cars stopping and starting, headlights big and bright
Nights getting colder, no sunshine light
Leaves on the trees falling down and around
Conkers on a piece of string falling on the ground

Ice on the morning ground like a piece of glass
Shining, sparkling, gleaming like newly polished brass
Looking out the window people looking glum
Waiting, anticipating, waiting for the sun.

Anthony Moore (11)
Sinfin Community School

CONFUSION

I have something to share with you
There is something I have to do
    To see, to find you're in my mind
  To hypnotise, to claim, to me this is a game
  A game of fame, not a fame but a game
  A game of death to be
  A deadly deal I have made
        I watch my step
I never know what or who will be
Waiting around that corner
               Behind that tree
I warn you
        I can calm you
           Harm you
Take this in because you or *it*
    You're non existent
             You're not there
Am I talking to thin air?
        I am confused!

Carly Wheattey (11)
Sinfin Community School

CASCADING WATERFALL

I stop to look at the clear cascading waterfall.
It makes a frothy pool of water as it hits the river.
Beneath the water there are tiny pebbles lying still as ever,
Fish dart around like speeding boats.
The water flows into a twisting river,
As it goes into the distance the river gets thinner.
A beautiful green forest surrounds the river.
Everything is wonderful, clean and green.
But,
The top of the waterfall has a rusty old trolley
And a bike wheel on top.
I shall go and get them,
The forest *shall* be a clean and safer environment.

Lucy Borrington (11)
Sinfin Community School

THE LONELY DOG

She sat there lonely, sad,
No one to love her,
No one to care for her,
Eyes glistening in the sun,
As if she was about to cry,
Her coat of fur like the rays of the golden sun,
A lady comes to look,
But takes the puppy next door,
She looks up as if to say,
'It's not fair,'
It's quiet in the kennels,
Until a child comes running in shouting,
'I want this one!'
She points at the lonely dog,
Her mum walks in,
Pays for the dog
'Let's call her Ellie,'
It's all quiet but no lonely dog,
The lonely dog is now a happy dog.

Sarah Weston (11)
Sinfin Community School

THE BULLY

The bully waits in the darkened alley
Ready, for his unknowing victim
Footsteps . . .
The bully gets in a convenient position ready to pounce
A shadow approaches, a foot, a leg, a . . .
The bully pounces onto his struggling victim
His hand over the victim's mouth.
The bully pulls the unfortunate individual down the darkening alley,
Away from the busy high street,
Hoping no one's seen what's happened.
The bully opens a gate,
He shuts it.
The bully ties a rope around the victim's hands
He ties a gag around his mouth.
Pheeee, phee, pheee, phee,
A whistle blows.
A mob gathers round the victim, intimidates the victim for money
He refuses.
They all pounce, *bang*.
Half an hour later the victim is released,
He struggles back onto the high street.
The victim feels in his pockets to keep his hands warm
The money, gone!
At last it is too much, the victim collapses in a heap on the floor,
People gather round
Ambulance, Fire, Police, *Ambulance*
Nee naw, nee naw,
Help, at last.

Annika Jenson (11)
Sinfin Community School

CATS

Cats play and sleep all day
They always look out for their prey
When they pounce, they jump so high
They could very nearly catch a fly

So they take it into their territory
And hide it behind the old settee
When the owners come home
The cat already wishes he was alone

All the children fuss over the cat
He wishes they could be gone like that
But deep down inside he's glad he came
Since a little kitten, he wanted to be in fame.

Emma Todd (11)
Sinfin Community School

SNOW

Soft snow has fallen
During the night
The grass snuggles under
A carpet of white

We climb in our wellies
Then button up warm
Make footsteps in circles
Around the white lawn

We roll up the snow
And make big balls of snow to stack
And build a white giant
A giant called Mack

When I look through my window
At night
Mack is just standing
Silent and white.

Kirandeep Bains (11)
Sinfin Community School